Julie Goes To School

in Signed English

Illustrations LINDA C. TOM

Text MARIANNE COLLINS-AHLGREN

Prepared under the supervision of the staff
of the Pre-school Signed English Project

KAREN LUCZAK SAULNIER
LILLIAN B. HAMILTON
HOWARD L. ROY, Consultant
HARRY BORNSTEIN, Director

Gallaudet College Press
Washington, D.C.
1974

Are you ready

for school?

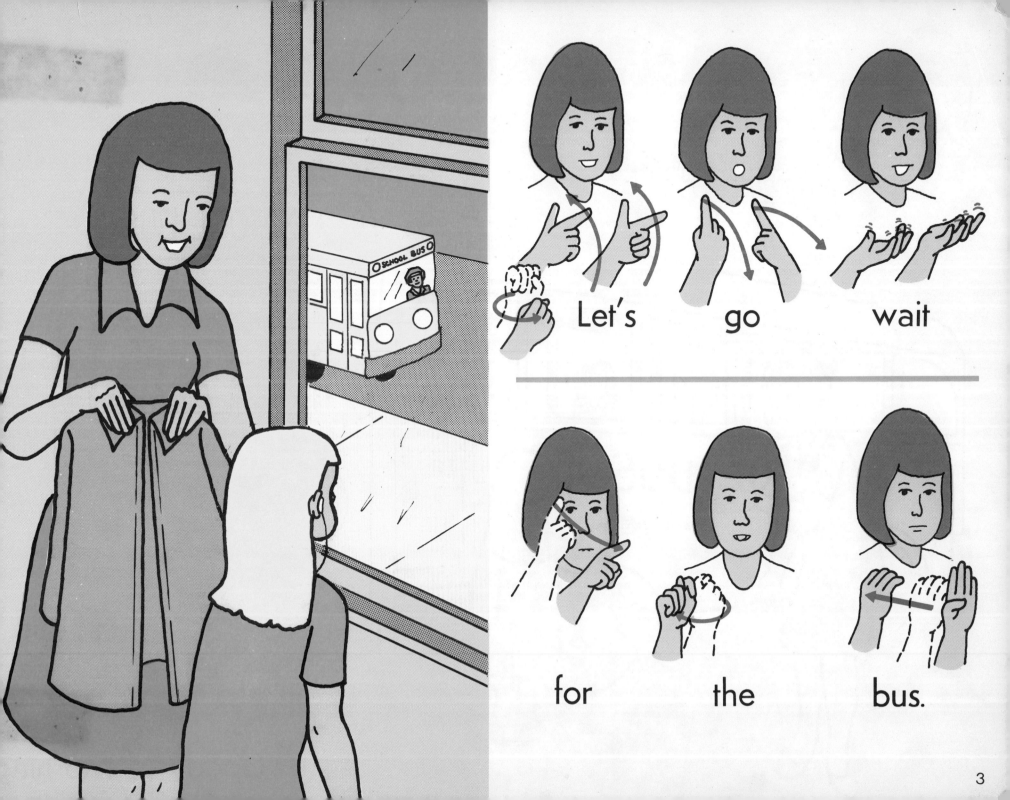

Let's go wait

for the bus.

Bye   Julie.

Good   Morning

4

Hi, come in.

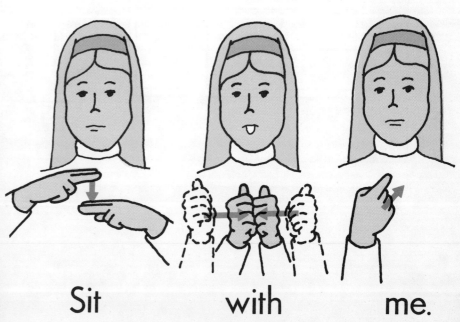

Sit with me.

SCHOOL BUS

Good   Morning,   children.   Hang   your

coats   up.   Put   your   lunch

boxes   on   the   shelf.

9

What day   is   it?

OCTOBER

S	M	T	W	Th	F	S
		1	2	3	4	5
6	7	8	9	10	11	12
13	14	15	16	17	18	19
19	20	21	22	23	24	25
26	27	28	29	30	31	

It   is   a   sunny   Monday.

Who   wants   to   draw   a   sun? 11

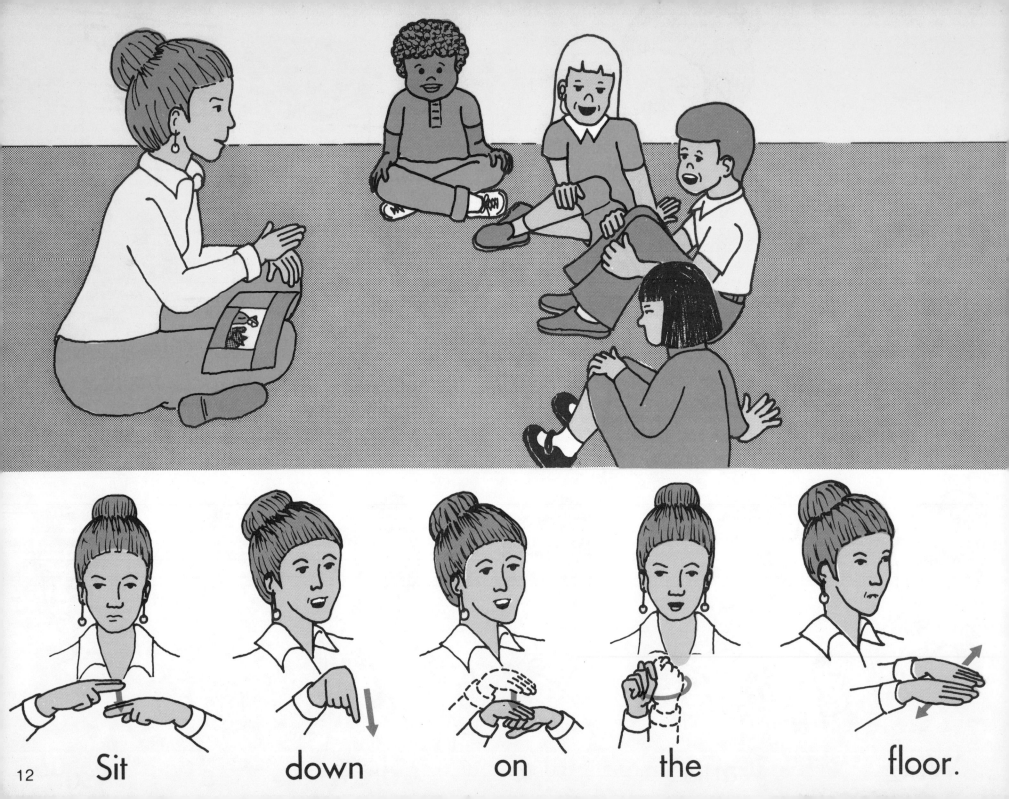

12 Sit   down   on   the   floor.

I   will   read   this   story   to   you. 13

14 Grandmother is afraid of the wolf.

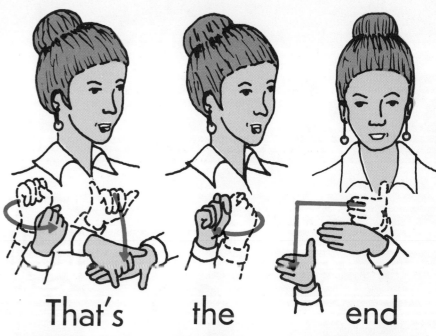

That's   the   end

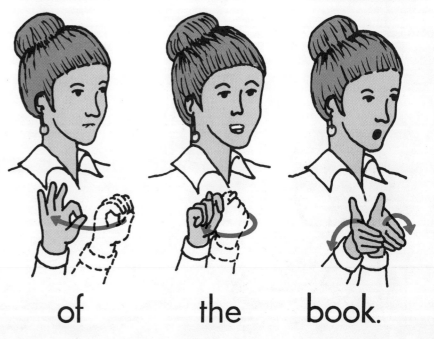

of   the   book.

Go   sit   down

at   the   table.

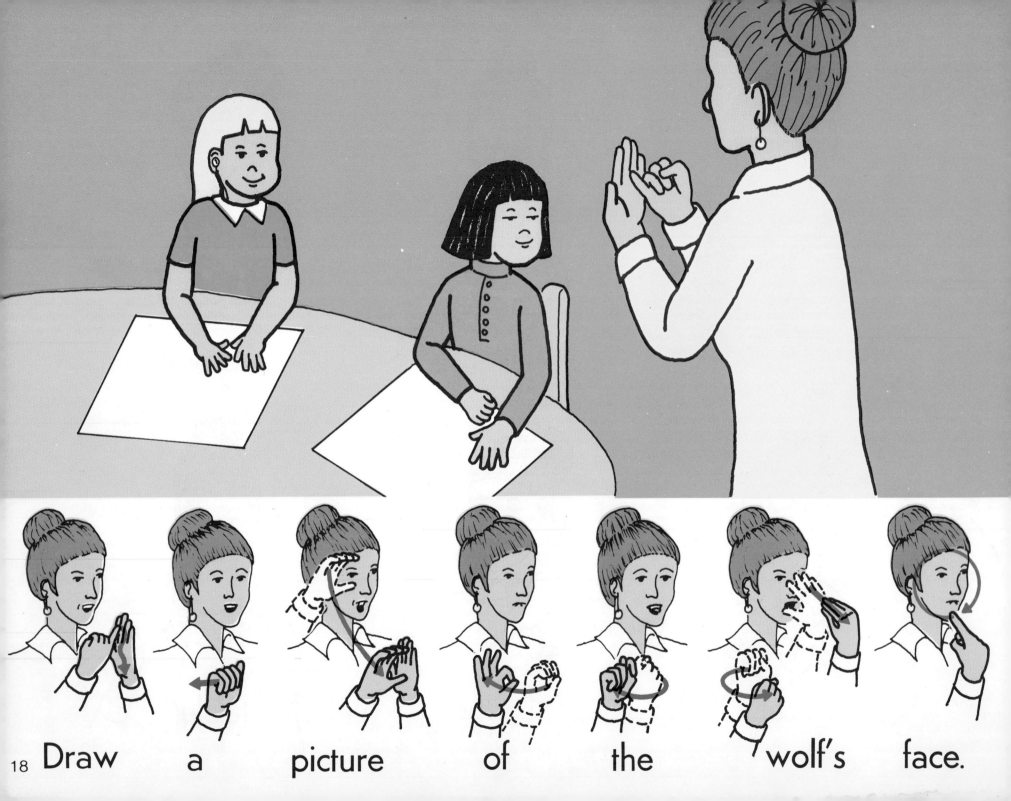

18 Draw a picture of the wolf's face.

Which   color   crayon

do   you   want?

Now cut on the lines.

Find the costumes. Let's

play Red Riding Hood.

We need a

grandmother, a wolf,

and a girl.

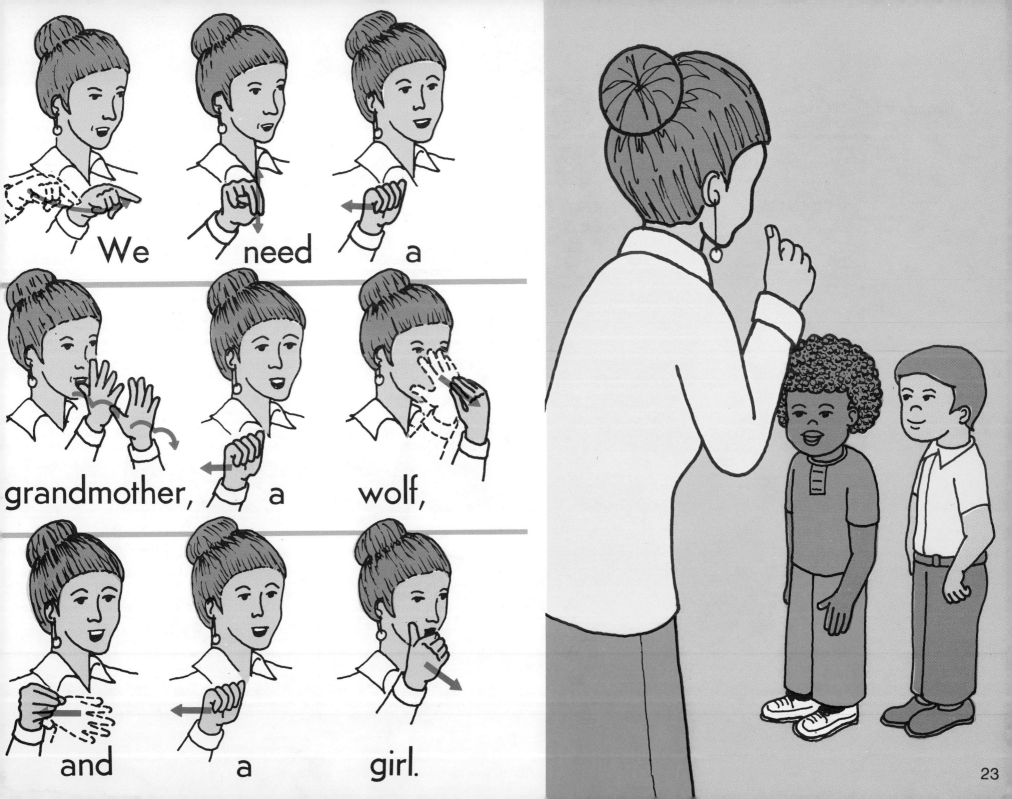

23

Who are you?

I'm grandmother,

a wolf, and

Red Riding Hood.

26

Please   share   the   costumes.

27

Are you having fun?

Take turns.

30   Come   back   into   school   now.

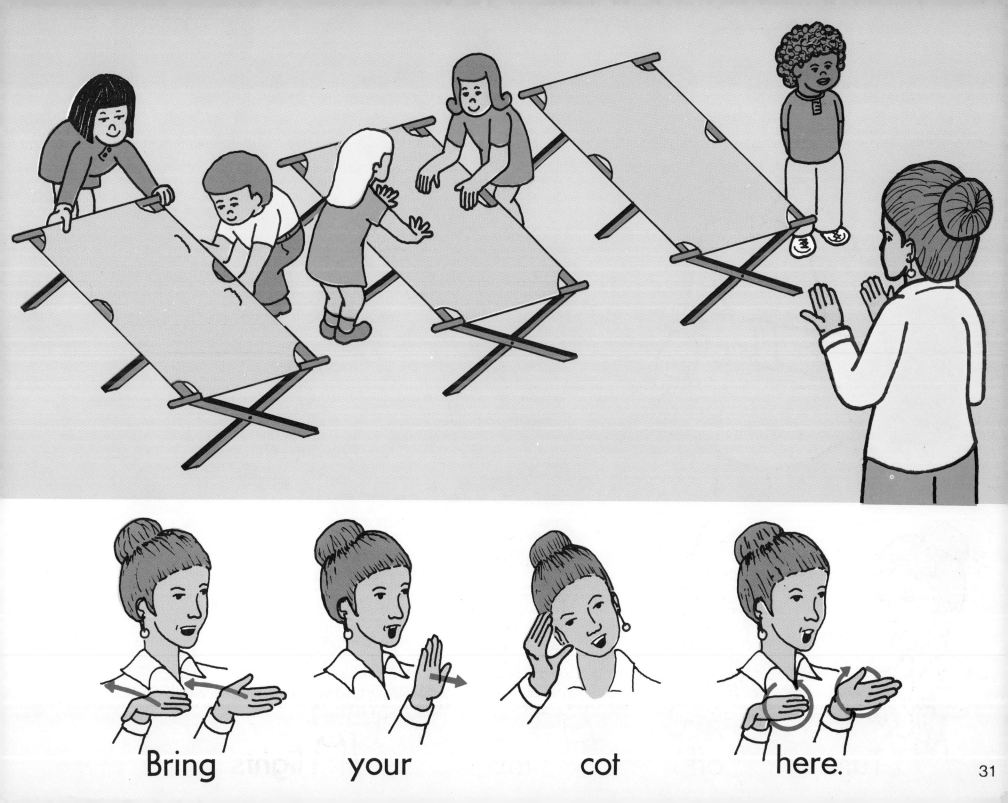

Bring your cot here.

Turn off the lights.

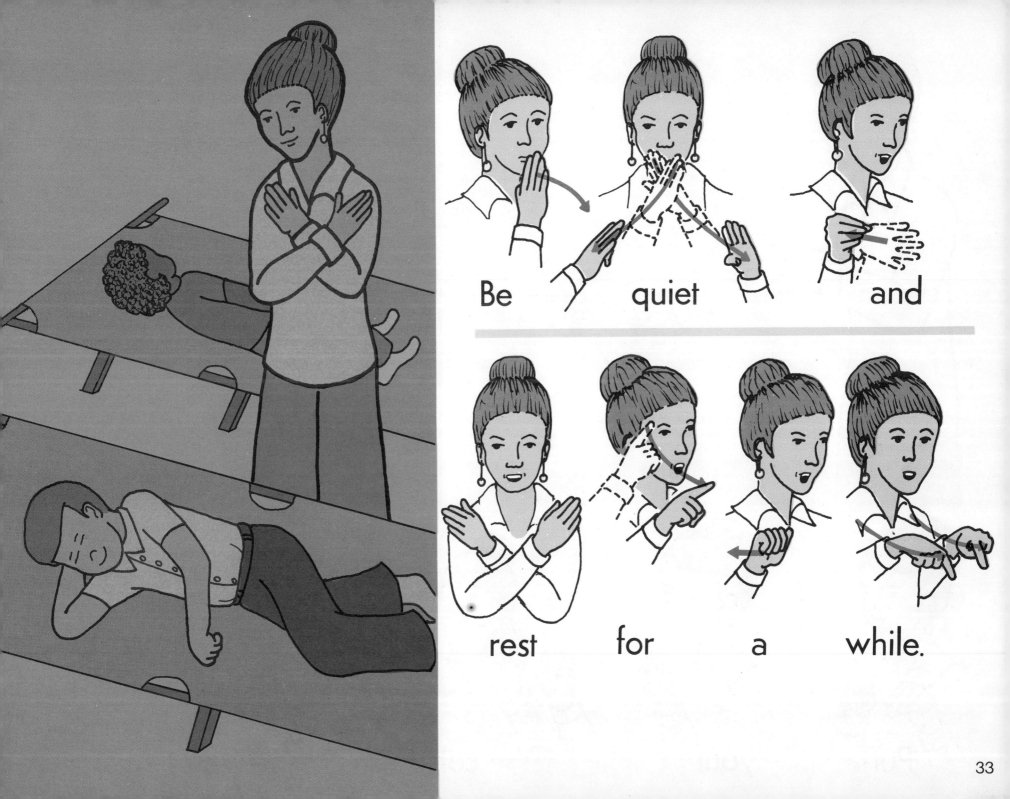

Be   quiet   and

rest   for   a   while.

33

Put   your   cots   away.

34

Can you all

see the picture?

36 Look　　　　　at　　　　　the　　　　　fireman.

Did   you

like   that   movie?

Would you like a snack?

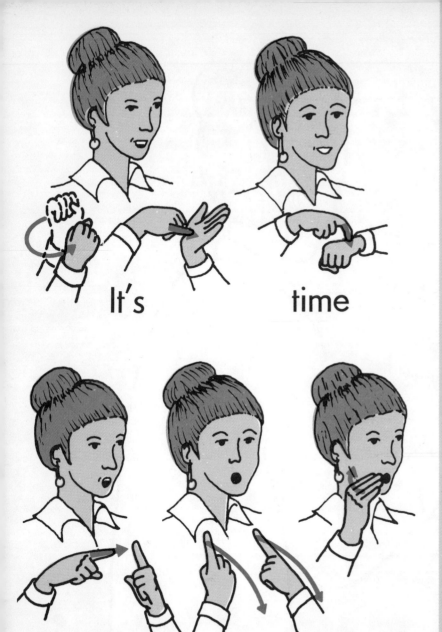

It's   time

to   go   home.

Put   your   coats   on.

Take your wolf mask home.

43

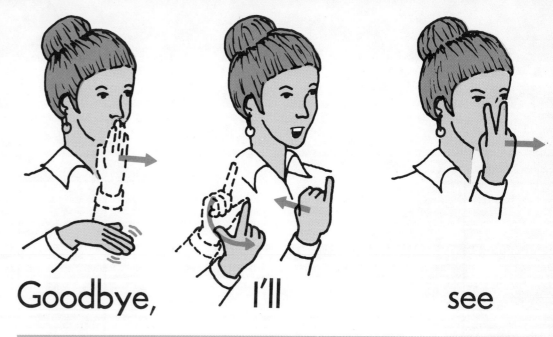

Goodbye,   I'll   see

you   tomorrow.

45

Index*

* First appearance only